Romans

SEEING THE WORLD
THROUGH GOD'S EYES

Marshall Shelley

ZondervanPublishingHouse
Grand Rapids, Michigan

A Division of HarperCollinsPublishers

Romans: Seeing the World Through God's Eyes
Copyright © 1995 by Marshall Shelley

Requests for information should be addressed to:

 ZondervanPublishingHouse
Grand Rapids, Michigan 49530

ISBN: 0–310–49821–X

Cover design by Jeff Sharpton, PAZ Design Group
Cover photograph by William J. Hebert
Interior design by Joe Vriend

Printed in the United States of America

97 98 99 00 01 02 /❖ DP / 10 9 8 7 6 5 4

CONTENTS

GREAT BOOKS OF THE BIBLE

Every book of the Bible is important, because each one is inspired by God. But certain books draw us to them time and again for their strong encouragement, powerful teaching, and practical wisdom. The Great Books of the Bible Series brings into one collection eight biblical books that distinguish themselves either because of their undisputed excellence or because they are perennial favorites.

The Psalms, with their poetic imagery, help us express our emotions to God and see the myriad ways God works during the best and worst times of our lives. Two books—Proverbs in the Old Testament and James in the New Testament—offer practical wisdom for dealing with the decisions and realities of everyday life. The gospel of John gives us the most intimate and personal view of Jesus, the God-become-man who is Savior and Lord.

Three books are letters written by the apostle Paul. Romans is Paul's masterpiece—the clearest and fullest explanation of the gospel found in Scripture; there we see our world through God's eyes. Philippians shows us how to experience joy when we are under pressure. Ephesians explores the crucial role of the church as a living community, giving us just a little taste of heaven on earth as we seek to serve the Lord.

The series ends where the Bible does—with Revelation, the last book of the Bible, where we glimpse our glorious future, when all things will become new.

Whether you are a new student of God's Word or one who has studied these books many times before, you will find here new insights and fresh perspectives that will make the Bible come alive for you.

The Great Books of the Bible Series is designed to be flexible. You can use the guides in any order. You can use them individually or in a small group or Sunday school class. Some of the guides have six studies; others have as many as thirteen. Moreover, these books help us discover what the Bible says rather than simply telling us the answers. The questions encourage us to think and explore options rather than merely filling in the blanks with one-word answers.

Leader's notes are provided in the back of each guide. They show how to lead a group discussion, provide additional information on questions, and suggest ways to deal with problems that may come up in the discussion. With such helps, someone with little or no experience can lead an effective study.

Suggestions for Individual Study

1. Begin each study with prayer. Ask God to help you understand the passage and to apply it to your life.

2. A good modern translation, such as the *New International Version,* the *New American Standard Bible,* or the *New Revised Standard Version,* will give you the most help. Questions in this guide are based on the *New International Version.*

3. Read and reread the passage(s). You must know what the passage says before you can understand what it means and how it applies to you.

4. Write your answers in the spaces provided in the study guide. This will help you to express clearly your understanding of the passage.

5. Keep a Bible dictionary handy. Use it to look up unfamiliar words, names, or places.

Suggestions for Group Study

1. Come to the study prepared. Careful preparation will greatly enrich your time in group discussion.

2. Be willing to join in the discussion. The leader of the group will not be lecturing, but will encourage people to discuss what they have learned in the passage. Plan to share what God has taught you in your individual study.

3. Stick to the passage being studied. Base your answers on the verses being discussed rather than on outside authorities such as commentaries or your favorite author or speaker.

4. Try to be sensitive to the other members of the group. Listen attentively when they speak, and be affirming whenever you can. This will encourage more hesitant members of the group to participate.

5. Be careful not to dominate the discussion. By all means participate! But allow others to have equal time.

6. If you are the discussion leader, you will find additional suggestions and helpful ideas in the leader's notes at the back of the guide.

Seeing the World Through God's Eyes

When Lloyd Douglas was a university student, he lived upstairs in a boarding house. On the first floor lived a retired music professor, now infirm and unable to leave his apartment.

Douglas, who would later become famous as the author of the novels *The Robe* and *The Big Fisherman,* developed a ritual with the old professor. On his way out every morning, Douglas would open the elderly gentleman's door and ask, "Well, what's the good word?"

The professor would invariably pick up his tuning fork, rap it on the side of his wheelchair, and proclaim, "That, young man, is middle C. It was middle C yesterday; it will be middle C tomorrow; it will be middle C a thousand years from now. The tenor upstairs sings flat. The piano across the hall is out of tune. But, my friend, this is middle C!"

Douglas and the old man realized the importance of finding a constant, a reality they could depend on, one "still point in a turning world," as T. S. Eliot put it.

In a day and in a culture in which changes flood over us, we need to distinguish the fads from the timeless. We need to know what we can count on. Simone Weil said, "To always be relevant, you must say things that are eternal."

The book of Romans is filled with that kind of relevance. It is an eternal book, describing God's diagnosis of what is right and true—and what isn't—in the world. It is also utterly realistic. Today there is a growing interest in and desire for spirituality. It takes many forms, from the New Age movement to transcendental meditation to Eastern religions such as Buddhism and Hinduism. But all are in one way or another creations of the human imagination. That is why the book of Romans is so important. It discloses the one true God's perspective on spirituality. In it we learn to see the world through God's eyes.

Romans is the apostle Paul's most complete statement of theology, salvation, and the purposes of God for the human race. It is carefully written and precise—and at times puzzling. Yet, although in places it is difficult to understand, Romans is also lively, full of surprises, demanding, compassionate, and breathtakingly epic in its scope.

Of all the books in the Bible, this one has perhaps had the greatest impact of all on the history of the church. Romans has profoundly shaped those who have profoundly shaped the church.

In A.D. 386, the brilliant North African professor of rhetoric, Augustine, sat in a garden and wept over his inability to break from his patterns of immorality as he tried to begin a new life. He picked up a scroll of Romans and read two verses from chapter 13: "Clothe yourselves with the Lord Jesus Christ, and do not think about how to gratify the desires of the sinful nature." He stopped.

"No further would I read," Augustine wrote later, "nor had I any need; instantly at the end of this sentence, a clear light flooded my heart and all the darkness of doubt vanished away." He went on to become the church's most influential theologian, shaping Christian doctrine even to this day.

In 1515 Martin Luther was agonizing over his inability to live up to his own standards—let alone God's standards—when he took up the book of Romans. "Night and day I pondered," he wrote later, "until I grasped the truth that the righteousness of God is that righteousness whereby, through grace and sheer mercy, he justifies us by faith. Thereupon I felt myself to be reborn and to have gone through open doors into paradise. The whole Scripture took on new meaning, and whereas before the 'righteousness of God' had filled me with hate, now it became to me inexpressibly sweet in greater love. This passage in Paul [Romans 1:17] became to me a gateway to heaven."

Two years later, Luther nailed the Ninety-five Theses to the door of the castle church in Wittenberg, Germany, setting in motion the movement that became the Protestant Reformation.

In 1738 John Wesley, who considered himself religious but found no joy or assurance in it, reluctantly went to a meeting where someone was reading Luther's preface to Romans. Wesley wrote in his journal, "While he was describing the change which God works in the heart through faith in Christ alone, I felt my heart strangely warmed. I felt I did trust Christ, Christ alone, for my salvation; and an assurance was given me that he had taken MY sins away, even MINE." This experience transformed Wesley and helped launch the great revivals of the eighteenth century in Great Britain and North America.* The influence of Romans continues, now, to you. My prayer is that you will find this book a means of understanding the transforming power of the gospel and of seeing our human condition from God's perspective. Romans contains many difficult concepts and confronts us with many questions about ourselves and our relationship to God. The challenge is not to understand truth according to our human logic and ways of thinking, but to try to see the truth through God's eyes. Then, as the brilliant Reformer John Calvin said of Romans, "If a man understands it, he has a sure road opened for him to the understanding of the whole Scripture."

---

*The material on Augustine, Luther, and Wesley is derived from F. F. Bruce, *Romans,* Tyndale New Testament Commentaries (Grand Rapids: Eerdmans, 1963), pp. 56–58.

STUDY 1
THE GOSPEL TRUTH
ROMANS 1:1–17

In recognition of your excellent performance, we'd like to give you a promotion and a raise."

"The biopsy was negative."

"Congratulations! You're the parents of a healthy baby boy."

"Your test scores were the best in the whole class."

"The war is over."

Good news seems to be in short supply these days. Perhaps that is why, when we hear some, it is so welcome and uplifting.

The book of Romans begins with the announcement of the best news of all: the "gospel," God's good news.

1. Describe briefly a recent instance of good news in your life.

How did you react?

2. Read Romans 1:1. If *gospel* literally means "good news," what does verse 1 suggest about the message Paul is going to deliver?

3. *Apostle* means "one sent with a message." Christians in Rome would also have understood it to mean a person with the authority to speak for God and to give leadership to the church. How does Paul's introduction of himself in verse 1 prepare readers for the gospel?

4. In his brief summary of the gospel (vv. 2–5), what are the important points about this good news that Paul chooses to include?

5. According to verse 5, does obedience produce faith, or does faith produce obedience? What difference does this distinction make?

6. How do you think the Romans' calling is similar to Paul's (v. 6)?

   What difference does it make that God's calling includes you?

How does knowing that God has a special assignment for you affect your goals, your priorities, your values, and your lifestyle?

7. Based on verses 8–13, how would you describe Paul's attitude toward the Roman Christians?

8. What "spiritual gift" can one Christian give to another (v. 11)?

9. Why would Paul, a well-educated Jew, describe his mission the way he does in verses 14–15?

   Why might he feel obligated to emphasize this point?

10. What about his situation might tempt Paul to be "ashamed" of the gospel (v. 16)?

    Why does he emphasize its power for everyone?

11. What tempts you to be less than eager to tell others about the gospel?

12. What evidences have you seen that the gospel is "the power" of God?

13. The word *salvation* has two aspects: (a) spiritual wholeness and healing in this life, and (b) eternity with God in the life to come. Which aspect has been more important to you recently?

14. Where does righteousness come from, according to verse 17?

How is this different from a person "trying to be good enough" for God?

15. Elsewhere in the Bible, faith is defined as "believing that God exists, and that he rewards those who earnestly seek him" (Hebrews 11:6). How does that kind of faith affect the way you face the events in your life this week?

Memory Verse I am not ashamed of the gospel, because it is the power of God for the salvation of everyone who believes: first for the Jew, then for the Gentile.

—Romans 1:16

Between Studies

Write a brief letter to an imaginary or real friend that explains why you are a Christian and why you would like that person to be a Christian, too.

Study 2
A Grim Diagnosis
Romans 1:18–3:20

If a doctor determines that you have diabetes or a treatable form of cancer, would you want him to tell you? Of course you would. Even though the news is distressing, knowing it is better than not knowing it. Understanding the condition means you can take steps against the disease.

The book of Romans also makes a grim diagnosis, but the news is necessary. The condition can't be avoided. Study 2 looks at the bad news. Then Study 3 will look at God's solution to the bad news.

1. Recall, if possible, an instance when you received "bad news," but later realized it was to your benefit that you had been informed.

2. In Romans 1:18–32, what is the root problem Paul describes, and what are the results of that root problem?

3. Why do you suppose Paul uses the word *they* in 1:18–32 to describe those under judgment, but in chapter 2 begins using the word *you?*

4. Romans 2 describes "respectable people," those not conspicuously sinful. What does Paul say about their relationship to God?

5. When we pass judgment on others, how do we affirm God's standards while condemning ourselves?

6. In what way are "respectable people" guilty of doing the same things as those they condemn (2:1)?

7. Many non-Christians have high moral standards and are "nice people." How would Paul make use of their own high standards to show them their need for Christ?

8. How do the judgmental attitudes of religious people affect the nonreligious?

Why does Paul say those attitudes cause God's name to be "blasphemed among the Gentiles" (v. 24)?

9. Many Jews believed circumcision automatically guaranteed their relationship to God. What is the difference between the sign and substance of that relationship (vv. 25–27)?

10. How might Christians today fail to realize the true meaning of baptism or Communion?

11. How might some Jews have been tempted to blame God for their own unfaithfulness and unrighteousness?

How would you respond to those charges?

12. Paul points out that the Jews had many religious advantages (3:1–2). What advantages do we have as Christians?

How have you benefitted from these advantages?

How are they, in themselves, not sufficient?

13. Why doesn't Paul discuss righteousness through faith (3:21ff.) until he has proven our guilt under the law?

Memory Verse There will be trouble and distress for every human being who does evil; ... but glory, honor and peace for everyone who does good.

—Romans 2:9–10

Between Studies

Pray for three people important to you who do not know Christ as Savior and Lord.

THE FAITH SOLUTION

ROMANS 3:21-4:25

Imagine that you are hopelessly in debt. You are hit by high medical bills the same month your car's transmission breaks down and you discover that the furnace in your home needs to be replaced.

As you look at these expenses, you realize that these far surpass what the budget can endure, and you simply do not have the resources to cover the overwhelming debt. For several nights you can't sleep for worrying what you are going to do.

Then someone tells you about a wealthy philanthropist who sometimes helps people in difficult circumstances. You call this man and describe your predicament, and he says, "Consider yourself out of debt. Trust me, and I will take care of your bills." You thank him effusively and hang up the phone.

What happens next? Do you wonder whether this man will really do what he said he would? Do you keep looking for other ways to get the money to defray the debts? Do you try to figure out "what the catch is"? Do you check with the man's office daily to make sure he is following through?

What you do depends entirely on whether you trust him. Our response to Christ's canceling our debt of sin is likewise a matter of trust and faith.

1. When someone owes you money and has not paid it back, which consequence are you more likely to focus on: justice (the amount that is owed) or love (their further financial needs)? Explain.

2. Read Romans 3:21–31. In what way are people hopelessly in debt before God?

3. How does God satisfy the demands of both justice and love in his relationship to us?

4. Verse 21 describes "a righteousness from God," which means "God's way of putting people right with himself." Based on what you have learned in the first two studies, why must this happen "apart from the law"?

5. If being considered "approved by God" depends, not on the law, but on faith, what exactly is faith?

    How is it different from "observing the law" (v. 27)?

6. Some people think of faith in general terms ("You just gotta have faith"), meaning a vague hope that things will turn out okay. How is that different from "faith in Christ" (v. 22)?

7. People who are hopelessly alienated from God suddenly find themselves "in good standing." This transformation is so profound that Paul uses three metaphors to describe it. The first is being *justified* (v. 24), which describes a courtroom defendant who is granted an aquittal. How should this aquittal of all charges affect the way you think about yourself?

8. The metaphor of *redemption* (v. 24) refers to a slave who is purchased and then freed. In what ways has Christ freed you from slavery?

9. The third metaphor, *sacrifice of atonement* (v. 25), refers to the Old Testament system of sacrificing animals to substitute for the life of the sinner. How does Christ's death "demonstrate his justice" (v. 26)?

10. Abraham is the first person to be called "God's friend" (2 Chronicles 20:7). According to Romans 4, what did Abraham do to become God's friend?

11. How do the lives of Abraham and David show that God does not accept people on the basis of their "works"?

12. How does Abraham in verses 18–25 illustrate the predicaments we occasionally find ourselves in?

13. What "hopeless" situations are you facing now that require faith in God?

Memory Verse There is no difference, for all have sinned and fall short of the glory of God, and are justified freely by his grace through redemption that came by Christ Jesus.

—Romans 3:22–24

Between Studies

Reflect on one situation or relationship in your life that you wish were different. Pray for God's strength and divine wisdom to know what you can do to change those conditions.

WHAT'S UNDER THE HOOD?

ROMANS 5:1–21

Most adults know how to drive a car. They know about the ignition key, the gas pedal, the gearshift, and the brake. But how many adults actually know what happens under the hood? When they hear something squealing in the engine, how many know where to look?

In the first four chapters of Romans, Paul has explained the essence of the gospel: everyone is a sinner and is thus disqualified to live forever with God, but through faith (trusting God) men and women can be declared acceptable and have peace with God.

That is the gospel simply stated. But how does it work? What is "under the hood"? Chapter 5 begins to explain what fuels our faith and how it works.

1. Name one or two items you use in everyday life even though you don't know how they work.

Why would it be good to understand a bit more about how these things work?

2. Read Romans 5:1–5. In addition to the primary benefit of the gospel—"peace with God"—Paul mentions some other effects in verses 2–5. What are they?

   Which is most important to you right now?

3. Perhaps suffering does not always produce the qualities that Paul describes in verses 3–4. What key elements are necessary for these positive results to emerge from pain?

4. How do verses 6–8 clarify our understanding of the kind of love God has for us?

5. What is the distinction between being reconciled through Christ's death and being saved through his life (v. 10)?

6. In verses 12–21 Paul shows the impact one person can have. How are Adam and Christ similar?

7. How is Adam's contamination of the human race different from Christ's cure?

8. Why did Christ have to die? Why couldn't God just wipe the slate clean and say, "All is forgiven," without his Son having to enter the world and be crucified?

9. Some people understand verse 13 to state that those who are unaware of God's laws will avoid judgment. Why is that not the case?

   What is your understanding of the verse?

10. Why did God want the trespass to increase (v. 20)?

11. How does understanding "what's under the hood" (the role of Christ's death in the gospel) help you appreciate and apply the gospel to a greater degree in your life?

Memory Verse Therefore, since we have been justified through faith, we have peace with God through our Lord Jesus Christ, through whom we have gained access by faith into this grace in which we stand. And we rejoice in the hope of the glory of God.

—Romans 5:1–2

Consider this challenge: "If you were arrested and charged with being a Christian, would there be enough evidence to convict you?" What changes should you make in your life that will let others know that you are a follower of Christ?

Study 5
Why Be Good?

Romans 6:1 – 7:6

Philip Yancey describes one summer when he was learning German to complete a graduate degree:

"How I hated that summer! On delightful evenings when my friends were sailing on Lake Michigan, riding bikes, and sipping coffee in patio cafes, I was holed up with a tutor parsing German verbs. Five nights a week, three hours a night I spent memorizing vocabulary I would never use again. I endured such torture for one purpose only: to pass the test and get my degree....

"What if the school registrar had said, 'Philip, we want you to learn German and take the test, but we guarantee that you'll get a passing grade. Your diploma has already been filled out.'

"Do you think I would have spent my summer evenings inside a hot, stuffy apartment? No way" (*Christianity Today,* March 7, 1994).

Substitute "resisting sin" for learning German, and receiving "God's approval" instead of a diploma, and you have the essence of the dilemma Paul addresses in Romans 6 and 7. Why be good if you know all your sins will be forgiven? Why live a holy life on earth if eternal life is already yours through God's grace?

1. What is one of the best gifts you have ever received?

How did the gift affect your relationship with the giver?

2. After assuring his readers that through faith in Jesus Christ
   they have peace with God, forgiveness of sin, and eternal life
   (5:1–21), Paul anticipates their response: "If we sin more,
   God will simply forgive more, so why not keep on sinning?"
   Before looking at Paul's answer, how would you answer this
   response?

3. Paul's answer is made up of three illustrations. The first
   (6:1–14) is death. How is our relationship to sin like our
   relationship to something (or someone) that has died?

4. In what ways are "sin" and "death" related?

   In what ways is sin self-destructive?

5. Why do you think Paul instructs, "Count yourselves dead to
   sin but alive to God in Christ Jesus"?

6. Paul's second illustration begins with a question (6:15): Just because we are not under the Old Testament law, does that mean we have no constraints on our attitudes and actions? Paul retorts, "By no means!" How would you respond to someone who says, "If grace is free, then I have no obligation to behave any particular way"?

7. Paul's response (6:16–23) is that everyone serves someone: Either you are a slave to your sinful impulses, or you are a slave to righteousness. How does it help you to know that you have a choice of masters?

8. Paul's third illustration is marriage (7:1–6). How does marriage illustrate the main point that "the law has authority over a man only as long as he lives"?

9. In what way does the law arouse "sinful passions" (v. 5)?

10. How does the "death" of the law affect the quality of our relationship to God?

11. In light of the verses considered in this study, how would you answer the question, "Why even try to be good?"

Between Studies

What temptations do you struggle with most? Pray for strength to resist, and consider what steps you can take to avoid them.

STUDY 6

WRESTLING IN THE SPIRIT

ROMANS 7:7 – 8:17

Nearly everyone at some point has said with dismay, "Now why did I do that?"

Whether we watch TV when we know a job needs to be finished or we turn our backs on someone who needs our help or we make a cutting remark that we know is both hurtful and largely untrue—we all do things that we would have to admit, deep down, we know we should not do. Why do people do what they know to be wrong?

What is more important, how can we change? Where do we get the power to live a life that pleases God?

1. Why *do* people do what they know to be wrong?

2. Read Romans 7:7–12. What is the relationship of the law to sin?

3. Verse 10 sounds as if Paul is saying that God's intentions for the law went awry and were unfulfilled. What do you think Paul means?

4. Why is it wrong to blame the law for our condemnation?

5. How or when can a Christian become immune to the power of sin?

6. Read Romans 7:14–20. Why is Paul so perplexed about his behavior?

7. What issues in your life have you anguished over as to your inability to live up to your standards and intentions?

8. What are the two "laws" that are at war in verses 20–23?

   What determines which side will win this war?

9. What benefits, if any, do you find as a result of the anguish you feel when you are torn by the war within (vv. 24–25)?

10. According to Romans 8:5, what is the essential difference between a person who is living according to the Spirit and one who is not?

11. Read Romans 8:1–7. What are the effects of living according to the Spirit?

12. Verse 17 could be wrongly understood to mean that a person must suffer in order to be one of God's heirs. Explain what the verse means.

Memory Verse The Spirit himself testifies that we are God's children. Now if we are children, then we are heirs—heirs of God and co-heirs with Christ, if indeed we share in his sufferings in order that we may also share in his glory.

—Romans 8:16–17

Between Studies

Some people claim to experience the Holy Spirit's working in unusual or spectacular ways. What are the ordinary ways in which you know that he is watching over you and guiding you day by day?

If you have a Bible concordance, take time to look up various biblical references to see what they tell us about the Spirit's work in our behalf.

THE GLORY OF CONQUERORS

ROMANS 8:18-39

I n sports there is nothing more exciting than a come-from-behind victory. Not many fans remember the games with lopsided scores in which one team dominates for the whole contest. But when someone hits the winning home run in the bottom of the ninth ... or throws a touchdown pass in overtime ... or sinks a three-point shot at the buzzer—those are moments of athletic glory.

The passage of Romans considered in this study also describes glory. It is not athletic glory in view, but eternal glory: the honor and celebration of receiving God's reward.

Part of the glory is that it is a triumph that emerges out of a seemingly hopeless situation.

1. What was something you had to wait and wait and wait for?

   In what way was it worth the wait?

2. Read Romans 8:18–25. What frustrates you most about living in a fallen world?

3. Who is the one who subjected the creation to frustration?

   How how does that frustration contribute to the purpose expressed in verse 21?

4. When was the last time you didn't know how or what to pray? If you can now see evidence of God's action in that situation, explain what you see.

5. Why would God intercede with himself (vv. 26–27)?

   What is the purpose of the Spirit's groans?

6. On what occasion was it most difficult for you to believe Romans 8:28?

7. Verse 28 seems to say that all bad events have good results. Explain why or why not this thought is true.

8. Notice the five verbs in verses 29–30 that describe God's process of transforming sinful people into eternal saints. How do you respond when you see the extent of God's plan to rescue the human race?

9. In verses 31–32, if Paul had simply asked, "Who is against us?" we could probably compile quite a list of adversaries—hostile forces in society, Satan, sin, death, and more. How does the way Paul phrases the question make these forces seem insignificant?

10. If an accuser brought us before the divine court, how would God respond to any charges made against us (vv. 33–34)?

11. Continuing the metaphor of a courtroom, Paul lists "the usual suspects," the things that usually cause people to fear that God is not blessing them (vv. 35–39). Why are these things not barriers to a Christian's experiencing God's love?

12. Overall, how would you describe Paul's mood in verses 28–39?

13. The next time you face hardship or persecution or danger, what truths from this lesson will accompany you?

Memory Verse

We know that in all things God works for the good of those who love him, who have been called according to his purpose.... In all these things we are more than conquerors through him who loved us.

—Romans 8:28, 37

Between Studies

What are some discouraging and unhappy situations in your life or the lives of people close to you that you have no control over? What would you like to see happen? Pray that God will change these circumstances; pray for patience and wisdom; and thank him that he knows all things and does all things well according to his purposes.

Study 8
Who's to Choose?
Romans 9:1-29

When you come to a part of the Bible you find difficult to understand and perhaps hard to accept, you have two choices. You can choose to interpret it so it makes sense to you—fitting the Bible into your understanding. Or you can choose to admit you don't understand it (and may not like what you *do* understand), and you subordinate your understanding to the Bible's teaching.

Romans 9 deals with the difficult issues of God's sovereignty and human responsibility. It is one of those Bible passages that test our understanding and our willingness to place ourselves under the Bible's authority.

The underlying truth presented in this chapter—that God chooses some to receive mercy and hardens others—may be a challenge to our minds, but to those who have received his salvation, it is a profound comfort to our souls.

1. After the soaring, lyrical climax of Romans 8:38–39, why do you think Paul suddenly expresses the anguish in his heart?

What is the connection between the two?

43

2. Paul feels so grieved that he says he would give up his own salvation if it meant that his race, the people of Israel, would accept the gospel of Christ. How is Paul's attitude a model for our dealings with those we know who reject Christ?

3. Why might some people think "God's word had failed" (v. 6)?

4. If the Jews by and large are rejecting God's offer of salvation through Jesus Christ, we might wonder whether God's promises to "his chosen people" are broken. Summarize Paul's response to this query in verses 6–13.

5. In what sense does God "hate" Esau (v. 13)?

6. From a human point of view, it can *feel* unfair that God selects some people to receive mercy and not others. How does Paul's argument in verses 14–18 oppose the concept that God's action constitutes injustice?

7. Suppose someone asks you, "If God deals with people selectively, how can he blame those he doesn't select for not selecting him?" How would you reply?

8. All those who follow Jesus are to be considered among "God's chosen"—that is, those sovereignly selected by God to be bearers of his good news of salvation. How does it feel to be handpicked by the almighty God for his special assignment?

9. If, as Paul says in verses 20–21, God has shaped us as a potter shapes clay, what are some of the key traits, attributes, and experiences he has designed in us?

10. What are the indications in your life that God has selected you to be a part of his purposes?

Memory Verse He says to Moses, "I will have mercy on whom I have mercy, and I will have compassion on whom I have compassion."
—Romans 9:15

Between Studies

Have you experienced a broken relationship, or have you become estranged from someone who is important to you? What can you do as a first step toward seeking reconciliation? Pray for grace and wisdom if the other person remains distant.

STUDY 9

WHAT HAPPENS TO ISRAEL?

ROMANS 9:30 - 11:36

When it comes to matters of religion, many people today say, "It doesn't matter what you believe as long as you're sincere." Or, "There's no such thing as absolute truth—you just have to be true to yourself."

Imagine what would happen if that kind of thinking were applied to medicine: "It doesn't matter what kind of treatment you receive—aspirin, penicillin, insulin, and chemotherapy are all the same—as long as you take them sincerely."

Or what if the same concept were applied to airlines? "There is no such thing as an absolute destination—Seattle? San Antonio? It's all relative—the pilots just have to be true to themselves."

Ridiculous? Of course. Yet people want to define their relationship to God on their own terms. In this section of Romans, Paul describes the reality of what God demands and how God defines his relationship with his people—and how his relationship continues with the nation of Israel.

1. Reflect silently on a time when you were close friends with someone, only to see that friendship fade. What caused you to grow distant from each other?

2. Read Romans 9:30–10:4. What caused the people of Israel to drift from their close relationship with God?

3. Based on Romans 10:1–4, how would Paul respond to someone who says, "It doesn't matter what you believe about God as long as you are sincere (or zealous)"?

4. Verse 4 is understood by some to mean that the Ten Commandments are obsolete. Why is this not so?

5. Compare verses 6–9 with the quotation from Moses that Paul cites (Deuteronomy 30:11–14).

    What is Paul's point about searching the heights and depths for Christ?

6. From a human point of view, what is required to be saved (vv. 9–10)?

7. In what ways are you letting people know that "Jesus is Lord"—specifically, *your* Lord?

8. In Romans 3:22 the words "there is no difference" condemned both Jews and Gentiles of sin and rebellion against God. How do these same words in 10:12 take on a far more positive meaning?

9. How do the three main sections of Romans 11:1–32 put boundaries around God's rejection of Israel?

10. On the basis of verses 20–23 some people fear losing their salvation. What do you understand these verses to mean?

11. On the basis of verses 25–32, in what way can you say that the Jews are still "the chosen people"?

12. In verses 33–36 Paul reviews how God works through nations and history to bring salvation to as many people as possible. What is his response? Make that your response also.

Memory Verse Oh, the depth of the riches of the wisdom and knowledge of God! How unsearchable his judgments, and his paths beyond tracing out!... For from him and through him and to him are all things. To him be the glory forever!

—Romans 11:33, 36

Between Studies

Based on your experience as a Christian, what would you tell someone who says, "We all worship the same God. It's arrogant and unkind for Christians to say they know more than anyone else by insisting that there's only one way to be saved"?

Pray for someone who needs to come to know Christ as Lord and Savior.

STUDY 10
LIVING, LOVING SACRIFICES
ROMANS 12:1-21

S uppose you had fallen out of a boat far from shore. The water was cold, and there was no way you could swim to safety. Your chances of surviving were nil—until a friend noticed that you were missing, went searching for you, and found you.

What do you think your relationship to that person would be after such an incident? The word . doesn't begin to describe the debt you feel.

Because God has rescued us from an equally hopeless situation, we too owe a debt of gratitude. In Romans 12 Paul describes the "reasonable service" we can render to the one who saved us.

1. Read Romans 12. Note the "therefore" in verse 1. What do the first eleven chapters of Romans have to do with the practical instructions found in chapter 12?

2. What phrase in verse 1 summarizes the main point of the first eleven chapters?

51

3. What is the significance of a "living sacrifice"?

4. How does the world pressure us to conform to its patterns of thinking and behavior (v. 2)?

5. Why do you think moral and spiritual transformation must begin by renewing our minds? How does this renewal take place?

6. Verse 2 states that doing God's will is pleasant and desirable. Why do you think many people have a negative impression of "God's will"?

7. How does being a member of a body (vv. 4–8) help us to have the healthy and accurate self-image described in verse 3?

8. How would you describe the particular gifts you have been given to help the rest of the body—that is, the community of believers?

9. How do the traits Paul points to in verses 9–13 help maintain balance in the body? For instance, what can happen to a person's "love" without "spiritual fervor"?

What often happens to "zeal" without "joyful hope"?

10. How do verses 14–21 help us get along with people who may be at odds with us?

11. How much should we give up to live at peace (v. 18)?

12. The image of heaping burning coals on an enemy's head is one of the most intriguing in the Bible. What do you think Paul has in mind in using this metaphor?

How do "burning coals" help to overcome evil?

Memory Verse Do not conform any longer to the pattern of this world, but be transformed by the renewing of your mind. Then you will be able to test and approve what God's will is—his good, pleasing and perfect will.

—Romans 12:2

Between Studies

Whom do you need to forgive right now? Plan to visit that person or, if that is not possible, to write a letter expressing your forgiveness.

Study 11

The Right to Rule — Now and Then

Romans 13:1-14

I magine that your boss tells you one afternoon, "We are closing early today. Take the rest of the day off—with pay." You quickly and happily head for home.

Then imagine that several days later, your boss says, "We have a special project that has to be finished tonight. I expect you to stay as late as necessary until it's done." You know you won't be home until long after dinnertime.

Question: Which situation requires you to submit to your boss's authority?

If you obey your boss's first request but refuse the second, do you think anyone would be convinced by your saying, "I'm a team player—I submitted the first time, and I didn't the second time. It all balances out"?

If someone asks you to do something you really like to do, is that submission? Or does submission mean being willing to obey even when you don't want to?

Paul's instructions to submit to governing authorities seem clear—but they also raise some questions for Christians.

1. What are services that government provides that you are glad to receive? Consider local, state, or federal services.

2. What are some activities of government or requirements it places upon you that you find hard to accept?

3. Why do you think submission to governing authorities is important for Christians?

4. Read Romans 13:1–7. What reasons for submission does Paul give?

5. In what areas of governmental authority do you need to submit more fully or more willingly?

6. Paul lived and wrote while the Roman Empire was at its height, at a time when the emperors were revered as divine. This makes his words in verse 1 difficult for some people to understand. Discuss what he means by saying that "the authorities that exist have been established by God" in light of the fact that not all governments have been benevolent or beneficial to their subjects' well-being.

7. It is believed that the evil emperor Nero was the one responsible for Paul's execution, although he was not the emperor when the book of Romans was written. Had Nero been the emperor at that time, what difference would it have made for Paul to write his words in verse 4 describing a ruler as "God's servant to do you good"?

8. How do you square Paul's instructions to submit to authorities with examples elsewhere in the Bible (Daniel 3 and 6; Acts 5:29) of God's people refusing to obey certain authorities?

9. Read verses 8–14. In addition to submitting to government, we are instructed to submit to one another in love (vv. 8–10). Why would Paul say we should continually feel in debt in regard to love?

10. Who comes to mind when you think of "a debt of gratitude" or "debts of love" that you owe?

11. Paul states that "the day [of Christ's return] is almost here" (v. 12). What effect does this awareness have upon our ability to love one another and to submit to ruling authorities?

12. As you look back over the specific injunctions indicated in this chapter, how can you "clothe yourselves with the Lord Jesus Christ" (v. 14)?

Memory Verse The commandments ... are summed up in this one rule: "Love your neighbor as yourself." Love does no harm to its neighbor. Therefore love is the fulfillment of the law.

—Romans 13:9–10

Between Studies

Are you using your abilities and gifts as much as you should in the service of God and the church or another Christian ministry? What could you be doing that you have put off getting involved in? Examine the ways in which you are serving the body of Christ?

Are You Strong or Weak?

Romans 14:1 - 15:13

Over the centuries, Christians have disagreed on all sorts of things. Consider each of the following, which some Christians insisted were helpful aids to worship and which others just as emphatically insisted were worldly distractions, making true worship impossible:

- Robed choirs
- Stained glass
- Professional clergy
- Incense
- Musical instruments (especially the organ)
- Taped accompaniment tracks

No, there is no shortage of issues that cause Christians to disagree with one another. And new ones emerge in each generation. Romans 14 and 15 offer principles to guide us when for conscience' sake we do not agree with the opinions and practices of other believers.

1. What is one activity you refuse to participate in on moral grounds but that you know other Christians do participate in?

2. What is something you participate in that some other Christians might consider immoral or unacceptable?

3. As you review the following list, imagine that you were planning to join a church and then discovered that every item is expected of every member. Mark each item yes or no (+ or–). Explain why you would or would not join the church as a result of this list.

— Giving a full 10 percent of your income

— Giving up something for Lent

— Having liturgical dance in worship

— Raising hands in worship

— Genuflecting in worship

— Practicing a simple lifestyle (used clothing, no jewelry, etc.)

   or

— Practicing a prosperous lifestyle (expensive suits, new cars, etc.)

— Hugging people of both sexes

— Kissing people of both sexes

— Undertaking a month-long mission assignment

4. Read Romans 14:1–8. Who are the strong, and who are the weak, according to Paul?

5. To what temptations are the strong vulnerable (v. 3)?

   To what temptations are the weak vulnerable?

6. How can both eating and not eating be done "to the Lord"?

   How can opposite actions honor God?

7. Does verse 4 mean we can never criticize those who don't agree with us? Explain your answer.

8. Instead of judging, what should be our focus with others who disagree? (See verses 13, 17–18, and 15:2.)

9. What does it mean to cause someone to stumble (vv. 13, 20) or to fall in the faith (v. 21)?

10. Read Romans 15:5–7. Explain how can there be unity in the community of believers amid disagreements on various issues.

11. How does Romans 15:7–13 draw together the main threads of the whole book of Romans?

Memory Verse May the God of hope fill you with all joy and peace as you trust in him, so that you may overflow with hope by the power of the Holy Spirit.

—Romans 15:13

Between Studies

What circumstances have disrupted—or threaten to disrupt—the harmony of your church or fellowship group? Pray for wisdom to know how to be a peacemaker and reconciler in that situation.

WHEN THE ROLL IS CALLED DOWN HERE

ROMANS 15:14 – 16:27

In Washington, D.C., in the grassy area between the Lincoln Memorial and the Washington Monument, stands a long, low, polished stone engraved with names—more than 50,000 names. Among its many visitors, some gaze at it quietly, some place their fingers upon a particular name, some make rubbings of names with pencil and paper. Parents point out special names to their children. Veterans in wheelchairs bow their heads in thoughts of the people who bore these names.

A list of names may not appear very interesting. But to those touched by the Vietnam War, the Vietnam Memorial is far more than just a list of names.

The centerpiece of this final study in the book of Romans is also a list of names. While you may not recognize many of them, these individuals and the work they did have left us a tremendous gift.

1. On what kinds of lists are you likely to find your name?

What is one list that you are glad to be included on?

2. Read Romans 16:1–24. After fifteen chapters of magnificent theology—covering the themes of revelation, creation, sin, justification, redemption, life in the Spirit, God's sovereignty, election, living sacrifices, love, governmental authority, how the strong are to treat the weak, the coming judgment—suddenly Paul becomes quite personal, describing his own plans and sending greetings to more than twenty-five people. What does this suggest about the relationship of doctrine and fellowship in the Christian faith?

What does this tell you about Paul?

3. What reasons does Romans 15:14–33 suggest as to why Paul sent these personal greetings?

4. What prevented Paul from visiting Rome before this time?

5. If Paul himself had healed the sick and even raised the dead, why do you think he asked for the prayers of these people (v. 31)?

6. As you look through the list of names, what strikes you about the way Paul commended these people?

7. After Paul commended them for their hard work, what concerns did he still have about them?

8. In what ways are we in danger of causing divisions and teachings contrary to the truth?

9. What aspects of the gospel does Paul highlight in verses 25–27?

10. Why do you think the gospel was "hidden for long ages" (v. 25)?

11. Now that you have studied the entire book of Romans, what has impressed you most?

Between Studies

Write a thank-you note or make a telephone call to three people this week, expressing gratitude for something they have done for you or for someone else. Include your pastor.

LEADER'S NOTES

eading a Bible discussion—especially for the first time—can make you feel both nervous and excited. If you are nervous, realize that you are in good company. Many biblical leaders, such as Moses, Joshua, and the apostle Paul, felt nervous and inadequate to lead others (see, for example, 1 Corinthians 2:3). Yet God's grace was sufficient for them, just as it will be for you.

Some excitement is also natural. Your leadership is a gift to the others in the group. Keep in mind, however, that other group members also share responsibility for the group. Your role is simply to stimulate discussion by asking questions and encouraging people to respond. The suggestions listed below can help you to be an effective leader.

Preparing to Lead

1. Ask God to help you understand and apply the passage to your own life. Unless that happens, you will not be prepared to lead others.

2. Carefully work through each question in the study guide. Meditate and reflect on the passage as you formulate your answers.

3. Familiarize yourself with the leader's notes for the study. These will help you understand the purpose of the study and will provide valuable information about the questions in the study.

4. Pray for the various members of the group. Ask God to use these studies to make you better disciples of Jesus Christ.

5. Before the first meeting, make sure each person has a study guide. Encourage them to prepare beforehand for each study.

Leading the Study

1. Begin the study on time. If people realize that the study begins on schedule, they will work harder to arrive on time.

2. At the beginning of your first time together, explain that these studies are designed to be discussions, not lectures. Encourage everyone to participate, but realize that some may be hesitant to speak during the first few sessions.

3. Read the introductory paragraph at the beginning of the discussion. This will orient the group to the passage being studied.

4. Read the passage aloud. You may choose to do this yourself, or you might ask for volunteers.

5. The questions in the guide are designed to be used just as they are written. If you wish, you may simply read each one aloud to the group. Or you may prefer to express them in your own words. Unnecessary rewording of the questions, however, is not recommended.

6. Don't be afraid of silence. People in the group may need time to think before responding.

7. Avoid answering your own questions. If necessary, rephrase a question until it is clearly understood. Even an eager group will quickly become passive and silent if they think the leader will do most of the talking.

8. Encourage more than one answer to each question. Ask, "What do the rest of you think?" or "Anyone else?" until several people have had a chance to respond.

9. Try to be affirming whenever possible. Let people know you appreciate their insights into the passage.

10. Never reject an answer. If it is clearly wrong, ask, "Which verse led you to that conclusion?" Or let the group handle the problem by asking them what they think about the question.

11. Avoid going off on tangents. If people wander off course, gently bring them back to the passage being considered.

12. Conclude your time together with conversational prayer. Ask God to help you apply those things that you learned in the study.

13. End on time. This will be easier if you control the pace of the discussion by not spending too much time on some questions or too little on others.

More suggestions and help are found in the book *Leading Bible Discussions* (InterVarsity Press). Reading it would be well worth your time.

The Gospel Truth
Romans 1:1–17

Purpose   To recognize the good news of salvation in Christ and to experience the power of the gospel.

Question 3   Paul's introduction lets readers know that the gospel is the good news *of God*. It is important that Paul was called and "set apart" to proclaim it. As a servant of Jesus Christ, Paul's special mission was to let people know about this good news.

Question 4   Paul points out that this good news is not brand-new; it is the same gospel that was promised by prophets in the Old Testament. Also, it centers in Jesus Christ—humanly, of a royal family line and a descendant of the great King David; supernaturally, the Son of God who died and rose again. It is for all people. And it leads to faith and to obedience of God.

Question 5   This verse indicates that part of the gospel is the truth that obedience emerges from faith. This has two significant implications. First, obedience—an effort to live a life that earns God's favor—is not the route *to* faith. Trying to impress God by our actions will always end in failure. Second, genuine faith leads to actions obedient to God. Faith is not just a statement we sign or a sentimental outlook that "everything's going to be okay." The gospel points to faith in God, and faith in God leads to a lifestyle of obedience.

Question 7   Paul's attitude is characterized by respect and affection. He longs to see his readers face to face. He sees great potential in them, which has already been partly realized.

Question 8   Paul's statement probably does not refer to "spiritual gifts" in the technical sense that he uses the term in 1 Corinthians 12 and 14 and Ephesians 4. Instead, "gift" probably refers to anything that contributes to a person's spirit. In contrast to a physical gift that can be seen and grasped, a spiritual gift is intangible but very real—a gift of encouragement, hope, purpose, significance, vision. Such gifts can build people's spirit and make them more effective in serving Christ.

Question 10   Prior to writing this letter, Paul had been imprisoned in Philippi, chased out of Thessalonica, smuggled out of Berea, and laughed at in Athens. Now, as he writes from Corinth, his message is considered foolishness to the intellectual Greeks and a stumbling block to practicing Jews. Yet Paul declares his unwavering confidence in the power of the gospel.

Question 14   This righteousness is something granted by God. In the Bible, the term *righteousness* does not mean "without fault" or "always doing the right thing." Instead, it means "acceptable" or "in right relationship." A person is "made righteous" by God's pronouncement. Like an immigrant being granted citizenship by his new country, God's righteousness is given to those who live by faith. Righteousness is not "trying to be good"; it is loving God and living as a faithful child. Sometimes even faithful children fail, but they return to God and seek his favor and forgiveness.

Study Two
A Grim Diagnosis
Romans 1:18–3:20

Purpose   To understand that everyone needs the gospel whether or not they recognize this or feel a need for it.

Question 1   Perhaps you were laid off from a job that, later on, you were glad you were rid of. Perhaps an unwelcome assignment became a means of strategic personal growth. Perhaps a relative became disabled or invalid, and because you were able to provide the crucial help, you forged a friendship you would not otherwise have had.

Question 2   The root problem is not recognizing God as our authority and worshiping him. When he is not the center of life, the logical alternative is a self-centered life, which results in the behaviors described in verses 24–32. Those behaviors, almost everyone recognizes, are self-destructive and lead to death.

Question 3   Paul's readers would undoubtedly agree with him that horrible sins are "out there in the world." After getting his readers to agree that some people certainly deserve judgment, Paul then begins to use the word *you,* showing that even we who don't identify ourselves as sinners are still under judgment for not living as we ought. Historically, it is understood that Paul was referring to Gentiles in chapter 1, but in chapter 2 addressed the Jewish Christians among his readers, showing them that they were not "off the hook" in being liable to judgment.

Question 5   We may understand that people are accountable to God and that God's standard is holiness. But we don't fully understand that the "respectable people" will also be judged for their actions and attitudes just as much as the more conspicuous sinners.

Question 6   Remember the sayings, "It takes one to know one" and "The pot calls the kettle black"? These proverbs demonstrate Paul's point: We often criticize others for the very faults that characterize us. In this case, both kinds of people fail to recognize their own guilt. They both fail to admit that God will hold them accountable for their sins. In addition, they presume to judge other people, which is to take on a role that belongs to God—and that is a form of idolatry.

Question 7   Verses 12–16 argue that such people, if they are honest with themselves, realize that they do not completely live up even to their own standards. They violate their ethical and moral ideals and thus fall short of their own "law."

Question 8   When religious people claim that God, forgiveness, and salvation are their private possessions, and when they snub or disdain other people who need forgiveness, they cause those people to give up on God and to ridicule the idea of hope and salvation. And this is not because they don't need God—all do need him—but because those whom claim to be "God's people" act like snobs.

Question 9   The value of the sign lay in reminding them to whom they belonged spiritually. But without faith and obedience, the relationship and the sign of it were meaningless. Like a man wearing a wedding ring while being unfaithful to his wife, circumcision without obedience to God is meaningless.

Question 10   Regular church attendance and observance of the sacraments are beneficial in helping us remember that we are sinners and in need of God. But they can work to our disdvantage if we think that by mere participation in church activities we will somehow earn God's favor.

Question 11   Paul points out that God is justified in condemning the Jews for not responding to God's means of salvation through the law, the prophets, and now through Jesus. They had the advantage of knowing about God through these means, but responsibility is the flip side of privilege. The more opportunity a person has to do right, the greater the condemnation if he or she doesn't do it.

Question 13 There is a difference between *description* and *prescription*. It is comparable to the difference between the doctor's thermometer and the medicine. What is the law—description or prescription? According to Paul, the law describes our dilemma. God's grace is the prescription—and that is the subject of the next study.

Study Three

The Faith Solution
Romans 3:21–4:25

Purpose To appreciate the splendor of God's justice, and to realize what it means to have a right relationship with him.

Question 3 Because of his justice, God cannot just ignore the debt. Because of his love, he does not condemn us for a debt we cannot pay. God pays the debt himself and gives a receipt: PAID IN FULL. God alone allows us to have the demands of justice met and to be "credited with righteousness."

Question 4 No person can be put right before God through the law, because no human being can keep the law completely and perfectly. Everyone is a lawbreaker at some time. If people are to be acceptable to God, it must be on some other basis.

Question 5 Faith is believing "that God exists and that he rewards those who earnestly seek him" (Hebrews 11:6). It is a profound trust and hope in Christ. Faith is the opposite of trying to earn or demand God's favor by works. Trying to impress God by works tends to make people self-righteous. Our trust must be in Christ alone—not our abilities to live impressively.

Question 6 Faith is not based on our ability not to worry. Faith is based on a confidence in Christ's ability to redeem all situations—good and bad—for the eventual glory of God.

Question 10 He "believed God"—that is, he had faith. He did not earn his relationship with God by works.

Question 11 Both Abraham and David committed serious sins even after they began walking with God. Abraham twice lied about his relationship to his wife, essentially offering her to powerful men who intimidated him (Genesis 12:10–15; 20:2). David committed murder to cover up his adultery (2 Samuel 11), and his relationships with his wives and sons were miserable. Yet Abraham and David were commended as men of faith, which should be an encouragement to all of us who fail at times.

Question 12 Abraham's body was "as good as dead." He and Sarah had no child and no hope of conceiving one. But God gave them a child. God has an uncanny way of bringing the unexpected to "hopeless" situations. Faith in God gives us courage to present him with the deepest longings of our heart, but it also gives us eyes to see his answers, even when they take forms we do not expect.

Study Four
What's Under the Hood?
Romans 5:1–21

Purpose To see that our everyday conduct and attitudes reveal how seriously we take the gospel and our salvation in Christ.

Question 1 Computers, automobiles, and electricity are among many possible answers.

Understanding the inner workings can inform us as to more or better ways they can be used. Such knowledge gives us a better idea how to repair them when something goes wrong.

Question 2 The gospel provides "hope in the glory of God." The word *glory* means weighty, solid, substantial. Like a fine marble chess set, a slate pool table, or a solid oak desk, the weight reveals the quality. The gospel places us in the care of a solid, unshakable God—a truly quality relationship.

But the gospel also allows us to "rejoice in our sufferings" because we realize that suffering is not the last word. The gospel allows us to see through suffering to perseverance, to character, to hope.

Question 3 For serious suffering to have any meaning at all, we must have a firm confidence that God is good, that he will overcome and eliminate evil and pain someday, and that in the meantime we are his agents to provide compassion and love to others who are suffering.

Question 4 God's amazing love was extended to people who did not love him! We were not only powerless to help ourselves, but were actually rebelling against him. Despite our being sinful and part of the human race that is in rebellion against God's authority, Christ died for us.

Question 5 Perhaps Paul is saying that if Christ loved us enough to die for us, now that he is resurrected and alive again, imagine how much *more* he loves us and can do for us. Or perhaps Paul is distinguishing between *justification* (our being declared free from sin's penalty because of Christ's death) and *sanctification* (our being increasingly set free from sin's power over our lives because of the living presence of Christ's spirit in us).

Question 6 Both have influenced the entire human race. Adam contaminated all of his descendants with a "genetic defect" called sin. Jesus provided a solution called salvation.

Question 7 Adam's contamination affects his physical descendants (every human being). Christ's cure applies to his spiritual decendants (everyone who accepts it). The gift of the gospel is available to all, but God does not force the cure upon unwilling souls. Salvation is for "those who receive God's abundant provision of grace and of the gift of righteousness" (v. 17).

Question 8 Justice demands that sin not be ignored. If a crime victim were told by the police, "We're not going to look for the perpetrator—why don't you just forgive whoever it was who assaulted you?" that would be injustice. God cannot overlook sin; otherwise, he would be guilty of injustice and actually condoning sinful behavior.

Christ's death shows the life-and-death seriousness of sin. By taking on himself the penalty we deserved, Christ satisfied both justice and mercy.

Question 9 Paul is *not* saying that some will get "off the hook" because the law of sin and death doesn't apply to them. He means just the opposite. The context makes clear that even before the law (Moses' law and the Ten Commandments) was given, sin had entered the world. And death comes to everyone, regardless of the extent of their knowledge of God's law. Verse 13 means that without the law, sin can't be spelled out, defined, charted, graphed, or *taken into account*. The law, like an accountant's ledger, allows for sin to be recorded for everyone to acknowledge.

Question 10   God did not want sin to multiply or for more people to sin. He wanted the *awareness* of sin to increase. The law brought sin out into the open. Our inability to live consistently by God's standards becomes obvious. God's law highlights our need so that his grace can be highlighted even more.

Study Five   *Why Be Good?*
Romans 6:1–7:6

Purpose   To experience the superiority of grace over law by avoiding sin and keeping temptation under control.

Question 3   We may continue to be influenced by something that has died (memories and ingrained patterns can linger), but it no longer has power to control us unless we allow it to. We are free to change.

Question 5   "Count yourselves" means to consider yourself a different person. Consider your old self, under the control of sin, to be dead—no longer the driving force in your life.

Often people trying to escape their past will stage their "death," wanting the world to consider them dead so they can begin a new life. Paul urges us to allow the old self to "die" so that the new life, centered in Christ, can begin.

In addition, when we place our faith in Christ, we identify with him, and Christ died to overcome the power of sin. Christ's life, death, and resurrection were all aimed at conquering sin. You cannot ally yourself with Christ and at the same time willingly support the adversary (sin and evil) that he died to defeat.

Question 7   Paul makes an apology of sorts (v. 19) for using this illustration. Slavery is not a positive image of our relationship to God. Slavery brings to mind a cringing fear of a cruel master.

But the bondage that defines slavery does not always have to convey a negative image: A train is free to run all over the country, but only if it is in "bondage"—a "slave"—to the rails. If it gets away from the rails, its freedom to move is derailed as well.

The truth behind Paul's illustration is that no one is completely free; we are all "under the influence" of something or someone (our past, our lusts, our peers, our ambitions). Paul says we are free only to choose whom we will serve. One master will lead us to destruction, the other will help us become the persons we were created to be.

Question 9 When confronted by a restriction, it is our human nature to say, "Oh, yeah? Who says I can't?" The natural response to the law is to get around it, an impulse which that in itself is a sinful passion.

Question 10 When we live under law, we feel trapped and oppressed because we are expected to live by a standard we are incapable of meeting. Even if we obey it outwardly, inwardly we can tend to become resentful of God and the law.

The "death" of the law frees us to be "married" again, this time to the grace of God. When we see ourselves free to choose, our whole attitude changes; no longer forced to obey, we now freely choose to follow God out of love and gratitude for his grace. It is the difference between a conscript and a volunteer.

Question 11 The first reason to be good is simply to consider the alternatives. If everyone does what he or she wants to do, society unravels. Even secular people are beginning to sense what happens when violence and greed and infidelity go unchecked. Events in Yugoslavia, Rwanda, Somalia, and Liberia during the 1990s provide sobering glimpses of the consequences of tribalism, anger, and revenge. A society without goodness will decay.

The second reason: Sin prevents us from experiencing God's purpose for us. He created us to become Christlike, and when we oppose that purpose, we can become frustrated and do emotional harm to ourselves.

The third reason: Intentionally sinning with the rationalization that forgiveness is available drains the sincerity out of repentance. The relationship is abused. Expecting God to forgive deliberate sin exploits his grace and insults the tremendous price Christ paid for our forgiveness.

Study Six	*Wrestling in the Spirit* Romans 7:7–8:17

Purpose   To understand what it means to live in the Spirit and act like co-heirs with Christ.

Question 3   Although the Old Testament laws themselves were healthy and life-giving, the total effect of them all was to show people just how pervasive sin and rebellion are within each person. God's plans did not go awry. He intended that the law bring life, and it does—by ultimately leading a person to recognize the poisonous effect of sin within his or her own life and pointing to Jesus Christ, "the end of the law" (Romans 10:4; Galatians 3:24).

Question 5   Not until the final coming of God's kingdom. Sin and temptation will continue to attack Christians until Christ returns. But Paul says that Christians have "died to sin" (Romans 6:2), which means that sin's toxic claim has been broken. Because the Holy Spirit lives in us, we do not have to succumb to sin's power; yet we must choose to resist temptation every day.

Question 10   The key difference lies in what a person's mind is set upon—sinful desires, or the life of the Spirit.

Question 12   The idea is wrong because that would suggest that Christ's death was not sufficient for our salvation—that something had to be added to what God has already done. The fact is, we will suffer if we are Christ's heirs. There are two kinds of suffering that Christ's followers will endure: (a) identifying with Christ as he agonizes over a lost world and his desire to reach it with salvation (Philippians 3:20; 2 Corinthians 1:5); and (b) facing persecution and rejection for our faith (Matthew 5:10–12; 2 Timothy 3:12).

Study Seven	*The Glory of Conquerors* Romans 8:18–39

Purpose   To see the sovereignty of God in every aspect of life and understand that he is in control even in our most difficult times.

Question 5   Perhaps the Spirit's groaning reflects God's intense desire to complete the process of redemption—it is as if he is talking to himself. But the main point here is that when we face difficult and painful situations, we are not alone. Even when we do not have the words to speak or know in what direction to turn, the Holy Spirit is pleading our case *for* us. We can be sure that the almighty God knows our situation and will redeem it for his (and our) eventual glory.

Question 7   It is not true. Evil and senseless cruelty do exist on this earth, but verse 28 entails three important qualifications:

a.   God is at work "in all things"—good and bad—to bring about his purposes. Bad things are still bad; death, for instance, is still an enemy of humankind. But evil is not the last word because God brings his power of redemption to all things, and out of death can come resurrection.

b.   This promise is for "those who love him." Those who are still in rebellion against God cannot depend on everything's being redemptive.

c.   The "good" that God produces is not the same as pleasure or convenience or ease. When God works for "good," he is producing a spiritual, eternal work that makes us stronger and prepares us for future glory with him in heaven.

Question 8   The implications of the words *foreknew* and *predestined* (and what they mean in connection with human responsibility and "free will") have been argued by Christians for centuries. But at the very least, *foreknowledge* means that prior to your birth, God conceived a plan of redemption that could save your life, and he knew that you would become aware of it (which is implied in your reading these words). *Predestined* means that the destination of this path of redemption is already established. If you get on this "gospel train," the track is surely going to take you to glory, where you will "be conformed to the likeness of his Son."

Question 12   There seems to be a growing excitement, an accelerating joy and exuberance, in contemplating the greatness of God and the privilege of being included in his plan of redemption.

Who's to Choose?
Romans 9:1–29

Purpose   To model our relationships with other people after the unconditional love that God has shown in establishing a relationship with us.

Question 1   A relationship with God is the most precious thing a person can have. But when friends and loved ones cannot or will not share that relationship, it causes tremendous heartache. Paul grieved over his fellow Jews who rejected God's love and offer of salvation through Christ.

Question 2   Many Christians are tempted to be angry and condemning toward those who reject Christ and don't live "a Christian life." While those people deserve God's judgment (just as we all do), they are not likely to be reached with the gospel through anger and condemnatory attitudes. To reach people, we must love them.

Question 3   If nothing can separate God's people from God himself (Romans 8:38–39), and if the Jews were God's people (a recurring theme throughout the Old Testament—Exodus 4:22; 19:5; Deuteronomy 14:1), then why are the Jews by and large not accepting the gospel? What went wrong? Paul here addresses those who are wondering whether God's promises in the Old Testament have been broken.

Question 4   Paul states that not all physical descendants of Abraham are "children of the promise." Paul's Jewish readers themselves would agree: The descendants of Ishmael (the Arabs) were part of Abraham's line, but the Jews never considered them part of the promise. Likewise, Isaac's sons, Jacob and Esau, were twins, but only Jacob became part of God's salvation story; Esau and his descendants became enemies of God. Paul's point is that not all of Abraham's descendants are heirs of the promise. It is just the reverse: Only those who trust God's promises are Abraham's true descendants.

Question 5   The point of this quotation from Malachi 1:2–3 is that God is free to select some people for his special purposes and not others. Jacob was hand-picked by God to serve in a particular way: His descendants would be "a light to the Gentiles" and bear the Messiah (Jesus) and would be the primary means by which God communicated the good news of salvation.

Esau was passed over for this honor. His descendants became increasingly wicked and eventually ceased to exist as a nation. By contrast to the special favor shown to Jacob, Esau was "hated." This does not mean that God was cruel in his treatment of Esau; it means that he does reserve the right to give special assignments to some and not to others.

Question 6   God's action might seem unfair, humanly speaking, but Paul shows why God is not unjust. True justice would mean that all are condemned for rebelling against God (see verse 22). God selects some people, deserving of destruction, to be redeemed. The issue here is not injustice, but selective mercy. God does not treat all people alike. But that is not injustice, Paul argues; rather, that is God's prerogative.

Question 7   Part of the issue here is a distinction between God's purpose and personal salvation. Sometimes we confuse the two concepts: Just because a person is not *selected* as part of "the chosen people" God is using at a particular time in history does not mean that individuals in that group cannot experience salvation. In the Old Testament, people such as the Syrian general Naaman, the priest Melchizedek, and the Moabite maiden Ruth were not among "the chosen people," but they trusted God and probably experienced personal salvation.

"God's purpose" includes saints and sinners, benevolent pagan kings (like Cyrus) and bad pagan kings (like Pharaoh), and miracles and catastrophes. God's basis of personal salvation is the same for every individual: trusting God and receiving the justification that Christ's death and resurrection provide.

Study Nine	*What Happens to Israel?*
	Romans 9:30–11:36

Purpose   To recognize that Christ is the only way to salvation, even though that is an increasingly unpopular concept in our culture.

Question 2   Israel related to God according to a misunderstanding of the law. They assumed that by obeying particular laws, they could build up a credit balance of righteousness that would obligate God to befriend and bless them. Of course, this did not work because no one can keep the law well enough to satisfy a holy God. The true purpose of the law was to induce people to trust and depend upon God—and to anticipate the Messiah, Jesus Christ, who would embody God's holiness.

Question 3 Those who refuse to accept Christ do not really know God, even if they profess to believe in God. Jesus told the Jews of his day that God could not be their Father because they did not recognize Jesus as God's Son (John 8:42, 47).

Question 4 The Ten Commandments express God's standards of righteousness, which remain in effect today. Christ, however, has "completed" the law. Certain elements of the Old Testament law (animal sacrifices, for example) foreshadowed Christ; such rituals are no longer necessary because Christ fulfilled the law. The law also made a distinction between holy things and common things (such as eating certain foods or observing certain days). Christ abolished this distinction.

Question 5 In Deuteronomy 30:11–14 Moses assured the Israelites that following the law was not too difficult; they would not have to ascend into heaven or cross the sea to follow the law. In the same way, Christians do not have to do heroic deeds to earn salvation. Salvation comes by faith alone.

Question 6 A continuing relationship with God is required for salvation. Even though sin broke this relationship, God provided a way back through Jesus Christ, the mediator who restores the connection (1 Timothy 2:5). We are saved when we sincerely believe Jesus died, rose from the dead, and is now Lord over all. If these convictions are deep and genuine, they inevitably are confessed by our words and way of living.

Question 9 Verses 1–10 point out that God's rejection is only partial; there has always been a remnant of the people that remained faithful to God. Verses 11–24 point out that the rejection is purposeful: It is intended to allow the rest of the world to come to God through Christ. In the metaphor of a plant, the Gentiles were grafted in where Israel was pruned off. Verses 25–32 point out that the rejection is temporary, that one day all of Israel will be saved.

Question 10   Some Christians believe that continuing to sin can result in their being cut off from God. Others believe that once people are genuinely saved, they cannot be lost; rather, they only *appear* to be saved, but actually are not.

But Paul is speaking here, not about individuals, but about groups of people. The nation of Israel on the whole was cut off from God's salvation by rejecting Jesus—and for the most part, Gentiles were those who embraced Christ. But Paul warns that no *group* can take God's blessing for granted. God can turn his attention away from Gentiles and place his focus back on Israel someday.

Question 11   God has planned a special future for Israel even though he has also now chosen Gentiles as his people. Because historical events have highlighted the Jews' ongoing presence as a distinct people despite severe persecution (the Holocaust, for instance), many believe that the Jewish people have been preserved so they will come to Christ (v. 26). With Israel's reclamation of its homeland, some also believe there will be a glorious national restoration of Israel under Christ (see Ezekiel 36:22–37:28).

Study Ten	*Living, Loving Sacrifices*
	Romans 12:1–21

Purpose   To practice Christlike mercy and forgiveness in our relationships with others.

Question 1   Only after we understand God's purpose and plan can we appreciate his expectations for our behavior and attitudes.

Question 2   The phrase is "God's mercy." Paul considers God's mercy his most remarkable trait. And for Paul, our most appropriate response is a life of grateful obedience. Verse 1 sounds the theme of this entire study of Romans; that is, "in view of God's mercy" means seeing the world through God's eyes.

Question 3   In the Old Testament, a sacrifice was something (an animal, a crop, a drink) that was given to God. It became wholly the property of God. But it was also usually consumed—either burned up by fire or eaten by the priests. Paul states here that Christians are living sacrifices—they are not burned or eaten, but they live their lives wholly as the property of God. Because God has spared our lives from eternal judgment, it is reasonable for us to live with the attitude "I owe my life to God." This "reasonable service" is a lifetime and a lifestyle of worship.

Question 5   The word translated "transform" is actually the Greek word from which we derive *metamorphosis*. A renewed mind can have a dramatic effect, changing us in a spiritual sense from crawling caterpillars to beautiful butterflies that can fly.

Question 7   By observing others in the body, and by their observations of us, we learn to appreciate the different gifts of one another. Moreover, we realize that we are not sufficient by ourselves to function as God's body, but together with other believers we can constitute a whole and healthy body.

Question 10   When we "bless" those who persecute us, we express a desire for good for them. Blessing and cursing are viewed as very serious matters in both the Old and the New Testaments. Although "blessing" enemies is unnatural to us, it opens the way for God to work in the lives of both us and our adversaries.

Question 11   Our natural response is usually to surrender very little when we have a conflict with someone. If someone makes our life difficult, we are inclined to fight or flee rather than figure out ways to live in harmony. This verse instructs us to work hard to seek peace. If our adversaries continue to attack, we may need to confront them or seek protection, but we do so for their good, hoping to win them over, not for personal vengeance (Matthew 18:15–17).

Question 12   Paul borrows this metaphor from Proverbs 25:21–22. It is generally understood that the coals represent the burning guilt and shame that adversaries feel when treated kindly in the face of their own unkindness. That combination of shame and goodwill can lead to repentance, reconciliation, and true friendship.

Study Eleven
The Right to Rule—Now and Then
Romans 13:1–14

Purpose   To develop a servant attitude and consider how we might reorder our lives in order to improve the well-being of others.

Question 4   Verse 5 identifies two reasons: (a) fear of punishment, and (b) conscience. While the former is clearly motivated by self-interest, the latter is more difficult to comprehend. Paul may have in mind the idea that Christians understand what submission and allegiance mean because their relationship to God entails complete trust and obedience. Submission to government is therefore a kind of reflection of our submission to God (see v. 2).

Question 7   Nero could hardly be called a servant of God. He persecuted Christians and viciously executed them. But in a limited sense, Nero did right when he punished criminals or maintained law and order. Paul urged Christians to pray for their rulers so peace would be kept and the gospel could be spread (1 Timothy 2:1–3). Paul no doubt prayed similarly for Nero. Still, God does not ignore evil. The Roman Senate eventually condemned Nero to death, leading him to take his own life.

The fact is, most of the emperors during Paul's lifetime had immoral and despicable lives. Yet their personal lifestyles seem to have had little effect on the governance of the Empire in general, which was administered under a very sophisticated body of law. The "governing authorities" comprised many persons, not just one evil emperor.

Question 8   When government intrudes into God's realm of morality and religion, believers "must obey God rather than men" (Acts 5:29). When Daniel and his friends (Daniel 3, 6) and the early Christians expressed civil disobedience, they were willing to suffer the consequences for their behavior.

Question 12   Even though as Christians we are already "in Christ" and Christ is in us, there is no room for complacency. The fulfillment of our commitment to Christ can be neither passive nor static. Therefore the Christian life is a continuing and continual effort to obey and become Christlike.

Study
Twelve

Are You Strong or Weak?
Romans 14:1–15:13

Purpose   To strive for peace and unity in the household of faith by considering the needs and desires of fellow believers.

Question 1   Some people might suggest activities such as smoking, gambling, consuming alcohol, wearing a military uniform, or worshiping with a particular style.

Question 4   The strong in faith were those who understood that eating certain foods (considered "unclean" by Jews or "immoral" by some Christians because the food had been prepared for use in pagan rituals) was not considered sinful by God. With the freedom of that understanding, they could eat those foods in good conscience (14:23). The weak in faith did not have that understanding; they felt it was more pleasing to God to abstain from these foods. Paul points out that if the latter had eaten such foods, it would have been a compromise of their convictions, a faith-violating act, and thus, for them, a sin (v. 23).

Question 5   The strong can develop an air of superiority and in disdaining the scruples of the weak come to despise the people themselves. By contrast, the weak can also develop an attitude of superiority in feeling that they have earned higher status in God's eyes by performing or not performing certain actions. The sins of pride and self-righteousness lurk in both attitudes.

Question 6   Both fasting and feasting can be means of worship. When an action is devoted to God and performed with a sincere heart, God accepts it as an expression of faith. Thus those who abstain from eating a certain kind of meat as a spiritual discipline are pleasing the Lord by their form of devotion. Those who eat that meat with sincere and grateful hearts, thanking God for this gift, are also pleasing God by their devotion.

Question 7   Criticism must not be mean-spirited or judgmental. Criticism arising from wrong motives or negative attitudes does not serve to build others up, but rather, tears them down. Constructive criticism—that is, criticism given to help the *weak become strong* or to help the *strong bear with the weak*—may require confrontation. But confronting can be done with genuine love and respect. Those who correct others will want to keep in mind their own shortcomings (Galatians 6:1). Yet also consider the example of Jesus: He was tender toward the spiritually weak, but not toward hypocritical legalists. Sometimes he flaunted his freedom before the Pharisees, deliberately challenging their sensitivities.

It is important not to regard secondary issues such as certain behaviors or interests as essentials of the Faith, as criteria by which we judge a person to be a Christian or not a Christian.

Question 9　Causing someone to stumble means leading that person to sin. If a person's conscience tells him a certain action is sinful, and if we influence him to override his conscience and to rationalize away his convictions about holiness, we have diminished God's authority in that person's life, causing him to sin (1 Corinthians 8:9–13). When a person's attitude toward God is soured because of the behavior of Christians, that person has stumbled and is in danger of falling (completely losing any faith in God). An air of superiority—whether from legalism or liberty—can turn people away from God and cause them not to place their trust in him.

Question 10　The goal is not for all to think alike or avoid all disagreements. The goal is to glorify God. We seek a unity in Christ that supersedes our differing preferences and personalities. Differences need not divide us—in fact, our diversity can enable us to multiply our praise and service for God.

Question 11　Among the themes we see in these verses are acceptance by God's grace through Christ, the sufficiency of the gospel for all kinds of people, and the joy, peace, and power that come from spiritual living.

Study Thirteen *When the Roll Is Called Down Here*
Romans 15:14–16:27

Purpose　To build up other believers by recognizing their contributions to the body of Christ.

Question 2　Some people consider doctrine impersonal or, worse, divisive. But understanding the mind of God and striving to follow his instructions are means to building close friendships.

No matter how admired Paul was as an apostle, he saw himself as one of a family of believers—a fellow worker and friend of those in Christ.

Question 3　Paul planned to visit Rome and hoped to see these people. He needed their prayers for a potentially dangerous visit he was about to make to Jerusalem before he could travel to Rome.

Question 4   Paul was called to preach the gospel where it had not been preached before. He was focused on "unreached peoples," and because a church had already been started in Rome, Paul had not gotten there—yet.

Question 5   Even though Paul performed miracles, he knew that everything he did was possible only because God was working in him. He knew how vital the prayers of others were if he wanted to maintain God's work in his life. Paul suspected correctly that certain people in Jerusalem wanted to harm him. He knew he could benefit by having others pray for him. Though circumstances did not turn out the way he might have hoped (he was arrested), God continued to work in mighty ways through Paul even during his captivity.

Question 6   Many were diligent workers, so Paul praised their hard efforts. Many also were slaves: The expression "those of the household of …" was often used to refer to slaves of a particular official. A significant number of these workers were women. It is interesting that Tryphena and Tryphosa (v. 12) were probably sisters, possibly twins—the names meaning "delicate" and "dainty"—but Paul commended them for working like "troopers." Also, Rufus (v. 13) may have been the son of Simon of Cyrene (see Mark 15:21), who carried Jesus' cross to Calvary.

Question 10   It seems strange that God would withhold information that could have saved many. The main point Paul is making is that God revealed himself in various ways through the ages (see, for example, Hebrews 1:1–2; Romans 1:19–20). Those who trusted in God—even before Christ came—were saved because of their faith. We don't know why God waited until he did to fulfill his promises of the Messiah and complete the means of salvation. Perhaps he delayed so that people would realize more fully that they cannot save themselves through their efforts.